The Low Country Shvitz

Rick Lupert

Savannah, GA, Charleston, SC,
Asheville and Charlotte, NC

The Low Country Shvitz

Ain't Got No Press

Design, Layout, Photography ~ Rick Lupert
Author Photo ~ Addie Lupert

First Edition ~ May, 2023

ISBN-13: 978-1-7330278-3-0

Visit the author online at
www.PoetrySuperHighway.com

Savannah is so beautiful that the dead never truly depart.

- James Sparks

In Charleston, more than elsewhere, you get the feeling that the twentieth century is a vast, unconscionable mistake.

- Pat Conroy

I came to this spot and thought the prospect finer than any other I had seen.

- George Vanderbilt

Thank you Addie, Jude, Brendan, Elizabeth, LB Sedlacek, Jeffrey McDaniel, The Jonas Family, The Thread (especially the Singers this time around), Our fearless Ghost Tour docent Ashley, Roger and Lydia, Carrie (The best bringer of pecan pie one could hope for), and Hydie the Charleston Cookie Lady.

Apologies to Cantor Ross Wolman who really wanted me to spell it *Schvitz*.

The poems "Caution, You May Get Wet" (page 9 with the title "It May Rain") and "Toe Eyes" (page 245) first appeared in *Interlitq,* December, 2022.

The poem "Opinions" (page 74) first appeared in *Stick Figure Poetry,* March, 2023.

For Addie who who makes everything possible.

Before go

and go

Caution, You May Get Wet

Addie says *there is a fifty percent chance
it will rain every day of our vacation.*

That's right, it's a vacation, so I hope you
appreciate that I'm doing all the work

of writing this book while on vacation.
I'm writing it for you. Speaking of you

I hope it's not raining where you are.
Unless you like the rain, in which case

I hope it's raining as much as you want it to.
As for me, although I understand the

southwest is running out of water
which is why we decided to let the lawn go

here where I am writing this book,
even before the vacation starts

because there's nothing I wouldn't do for you.
I think I lost track of where that last sentence

was going. I hope to take time away from
writing things down to lose track of things.

Anyway, I prefer it not to rain, but we'll
pack umbrellas just in case.

I Want to Get Wet

We dropped Jude off at camp two days ago.
There's a consistent quiet in our house
which I appreciate, but am not used to.

We saw a picture of him wearing white
with his arms around similarly dressed teens.
This is the time when their arms start

to get busy with each other.
We're hoping to fly away on Sunday
(It is Saturday in case you're making a timeline)

but there are tests to be done, and,
depending on their results, we may
cancel everything. Jay, who lives in Chicago

and is afraid of holes, says their camp requires
you to be six hours away in case it all goes to hell.
Savannah, Georgia will take longer to return from

in case it all goes to hell.
I'm praying for Georgian rain
to land on my head.

Better Pack a Lunch

I've been researching fine dining
vegetarian restaurants in Savannah,

Charleston and Asheville.
So far it feels like I'm ten years late

to the gold rush. I've got my mouth with me
but the river is empty.

Alone at Last

Even though Jude is at camp
we still keep the bedroom door
only slightly open at night
so the cats can get in and out
and we have some privacy from
the memory of him walking
down the hallway.

Opposites Attract

When Addie packs
it's a multi day affair
involving fashion shows
and endless decisions.

When I pack, I throw
some of my shit into
a suitcase a few hours
before we leave and

pray to God I can buy
a toothbrush in Georgia
in case it all goes to hell.

(Cream / Sugar)

The person at Starbucks asked me
three times if I wanted cream and sugar.
I guess she really wanted to know.
And look at me assuming
someone's pronouns again.

Holy Holy Holy

When getting out of the car
the coffee, which I mentioned
in the previous poem, spilled
out of the mouth hole and
onto my bare left knee.
It's too close to departure
to ready my legal machine
to deal with this. But it does
highlight one of the many
problems with holes.

Our Lyft driver

seems unsure of himself
his car, the road ahead of him.
I'd give him a hug but
this is not the time.

I'm Too Tired to Write Poems This Morning

I got the exact amount of sleep I'd need
if I was the opposite of a cat.

The car bounces up and down
(which is nice in case there are people

with you who prefer one over the other.)
More than occasionally the tires

remind us of the boundaries between lanes.
He could be a doctor or an engineer

where he came from, but again,
I am assuming too much.

5 7 5

This mask too tight on
my face. My head grown so big
since all this began.

The Past Is Still Here

They're working on technology
to allow us to store our IDs
on our phones. It's not here
for us yet so soon we'll have to
show our driver's licenses to
the agents like the cave men did
when they traveled.

Still In the Car
To The Airport

The driver ignores
the GPS instructions
like they've been married
for far too long.

P.S. I will forever do
whatever Addie says.

Don't Tell Anyone

I don't think I'm giving away
any great medical secret when
I tell you Addie just told me
her toe hurts..

In Flight

I
Addie notices my mask is on
upside down and she tells me
because she is here for me
which she also tells me.

Upside down masks –
They're the downed zipper
of our day.

II
We're sitting in the front row
of the plane which always makes
a short person like me feel better
about potentially obstructed views.

III
With enough gumption
I could have this whole book written
by the time we land.

IV
Water or orange juice *for now*
says *our* flight attendant
implying there's more to come.

V
Addie is pleased with the symmetrical
arrangement of our two coffee cups
and the two water cups. I expect
a great deal of *appreciated geometry*
over the next two weeks.

VI
The flight attendant announces
we will be flying at 33,000 feet.
The pilot had already said
it would be 35,000 feet.
Hopefully This 2,000 foot discrepancy
won't lead to fisticuffs between
the two of them.

VII
The clouds over
the Pacific Ocean
prevent me from seeing
the Pacific Ocean
but I truly believe
it is still there.

VIII
Noise canceling
is a feature I would like
in many other situations.

IX
33,000 feet
(if he is to be trusted)
can't come fast enough
to meet my desire
to explore the
First Class lavatory.
Here come the hot towels.

X
Masks are not required
and the pilot (Mister 35,000 feet)
asks us to not judge anyone's choice.
A couple boarding the plane
nod with maskless validation
upon hearing this and I
want to judge them, but they
have a cat with them so
they can't be that bad.

XI
The love of my life has lost
a first class blueberry
somewhere in her seat
just as we reach cruising altitude
but the rainbow order of the
given fruit distracts her
from this crisis.

XII
The meal comes with butter
which has us all wondering if
a bread basket is coming.

XIII
We spy on the hot breakfasts
behind us as, for some reason,
we have chosen the fruit and yogurt plate.

XIV
I think my reason is we are heading
to the southeast where it's going to
be a long stretch of one biscuit
after another.

XV
I hold up the butter and the knife
whenever he walks by, indicating
I am ready for the existence
of the bread basket.

XVI
The bread basket comes!
It includes biscuits which
the flight attendant refers to
as muffins. Apparently he skipped
the bread identifying class
at flight attendant school.

XVII
Addie makes a family of
origami birds which she
delights in positioning
all over the tray table.

XVIII
An hour and a half into this flight
and it is still a half hour before
I normally wake up. Sorry
for making you do math.

XIX
If anyone knows
where we're having dinner tonight
I'll kiss your hat.

XX
And then a whole series
of text messages riffing on
Charlotte, North Carolina's
airport code which will not
be duplicated here for the
sake of the children.

XXI
Addie is deeply invested in
the missing unaccompanied minor
who has yet to board the plane.
We are privy to all the details
from our perch in the front row.
The doors are closed and we're
already in airplane mode so
when they decide to reopen them
to let her on, in Addie's experience,
it's like all the rules of aviation
have been rewritten.
The airline employee who
escorted the young girl on
had a clear backpack with
a visible stock of crayons and
colored pencils and hidden things
we'd imagine would serve
to delight a child of any age.
So that's what the $150 goes to
Addie thinks, remembering the
one time we almost sent Jude
across the country all by himself.

In Flight, But a Different One

It's only a thirty-eight minute flight to Savannah
and I don't think the flight attendants
are taking it seriously. There's a lot of
frivolous cross checking and nothing
seems to be strapped in.
I hear them giggling. Thirty eight minutes?
Does it count?
Are we even going anywhere?

A night in
Savannah

Tear It Down, Just For Us

All of Broughton Street is under construction
as is the habit of cities when Luperts
come to visit.

The Force Is With Them

The Asian family
also waiting outside
Flying Monk Noodle Bar
has the Star Wars theme
emanating out of their phones
I assume in solidarity with my
Millennium Falcon T-shirt
and not simply to
placate their children.

Shvitz with Fritz

I tell Addie we're going to meet Fritz
tomorrow, our guide on the
40 Acres and a Mule Tour.
Keying in on the humidity
she asks if we're going to
shvitz with Fritz.
Oh, Addie, if you hadn't already
solidified your place in my life and work
this would have sealed the deal.

Yiddish

I
Much of this experience will be spent
determining whether it's spelled *shvitz*
or *schvitz*.

II
While we still don't have an answer
it has been put forth (by me) that
you know a word is Yiddish because
it sounds made up, but somehow,
you automatically know what it means.

According to a sign

in the back of *Flying Monk Noodle Bar*
an Apple was recently employee of the month.

Way to go, apple!

And way to go, *Flying Monk Noodle Bar*
for extending your inclusivity to
the fruit kingdom.

Zzzzzz

At the restaurant I tell Addie
my leg has definitely fallen asleep.
She pauses for a while and as soon
as she starts to say something
I interrupt her with *shhh you'll wake it up!*

Caution Without Knowledge

I sign up from River Street says
Historic Steps - Use At Own Risk.
Addie refuses to use the historic steps
until we learn more about their back story.

Hush Up

Instead of *Do Not Disturb*
the sign on our hotel door says
Hush Up. That's so southern
I want to shout it from the roof
but the sign's already up so I won't.

Initial Impression

Savannah is better closer to the river.
At least for people who don't live here.
It doesn't help that they've torn up
Broughton Street which was
our first destination and the furthest
from the river we've been.
Unless you count Los Angeles which
is *very* far from the river, this river.

This river, the Savannah River –
Cross it and you're in the Carolinas.
Walk along it and you'll find
everyone else – all of them.

We happened upon a people circus
a candy store, and I've already mentioned
the risky historic steps.
We hope to learn their story so
we can ascend them with a sense of that weight.
If we were smart we might descend them instead.

The cobblestones, the lingering scent
of the Revolutionary War and
the funk of slavery.

Tomorrow, according to the pattern
we've grown accustomed to
is another day.
It's *forty acres and a mule* day,
It's Fritz day.

If the line isn't too long it'll start with a biscuit
and coffee, those who came before me
described as fabulous.
But not now, not this moment.
There is so much to sleep
before I shvitz.

Savannah
Day 1

Weather Report From Addie:

It's humid today.
Current temperature 80 degrees.
Real feel: shut the fuck up.

I'm At It Again

I saw a sign that said *Hiring all Positions*
I lay on the ground in front of the store and
lift up just one of my legs hoping for the
best possible salary.

Shvitzing With Fritz

Children we all shall be free –
Music emanates from Fritz's bag
as we walk on what used to be a dirt road.

A slave market on City Market
is now the Woof Gang Bakery
Neighborhood Pet Store –
The puppies and kittens
crying for the freedom of
new laps.

Black and white spirits
would meet in Ellis square
half way between the oldest black
and the oldest white churches.

Ellis Square was replaced by a parking lot
and then by a new Ellis Square.

The guns jarred the earth for miles
is how Susie Baker remembered
the artillery striking Fort Pulaski.

If the Yankees did take all my money
they did free our race. I will leave it
in God's hands.
                    ~Dolly Reed

Old punks in Ellis Square –
Their bodies have aged.
Their attitudes haven't.

Fritz plays music as we move
from square to square.
We move to Johnson Square
to *Moving Along*.

Fritz wants me to write down
Mulberry Plantation as he talks to us
in Johnson Square where Savannah
and Georgia began.

It's all about the cotton.

This whole thing is a play
that Fritz and his wife wrote.
It's like *Hamilton* except less expensive.

The oak trees in Johnson Square
are everything we've ever wanted
from trees.

The weeping time –
The largest sale of humans
during slave times.

Fritz has organized the trip so it gets
Closer and closer to his house and
farther and farther from our hotel.
This will be reflected in his tip.

Savannah is known as *Slowvannah*
but when it came to making a railroad
they got right on it.

Tomachichi was the leader
of the Yamacraw

Tomachichi is buried in Wright Square
right under the Gordon monument.

Charley Lamar was a fire eater.

The *Wanderer Affair* led to nothing
but Charles Lamar partying in his office.
He was the last conspicuous man
Killed in the civil war.

Georgia, named for King George II
was meant to be a land of agrarian equality
for England's righteous poor
free of slaves, a land of silk and wine.

Oglethorpe made the squares.
Went back to England.
Lost the battle to keep Georgia free.
Slavery called *a necessary evil.*

Georgia needed the expertise of the
West African rice cultivators.

We take a much needed facilities break.

A sign on the toilet says
*hold the handle down
and then it will work nice.*
This Southern hospitality
knows now bounds.

At Gallery Espresso

I
Addie orders a *Peach Honey Bush*.
Sadly, it's just a beverage.

II
If anyone is concerned about
the sweetness of the sweet tea
let me assure you, you should not be.

III
I ask for a lemon wedge
I need to *northern it up* a bit.

Some of Us Are Not in a Hurry

We walk into a CVS and
concerned about the time we have
until we tour the Sorrel Weed House
I tell Addie we have ninety seconds.
At my eighty-three seconds update it's clear
my deadlines are of no importance to her.

Matching Shirts

Addie and I are wearing matching
red white and blue pin striped shirts
as orchestrated by Old Navy and
the old man outside our hotel
wearing the same shirt who smiled
and said *Old Navy special* making him
the coolest grandpa in the south.

At the Historic
Sorrel Weed House

I
We ask if they have a restroom
and they point us to the modern hotel
across the street. I tell them I was hoping
for an *historic bathroom* and then
pause with my most serious looks
which is pretty serious and
has the desired effect.

II
You can see the fingerprints of the slaves
who made these courtyard bricks

III
We learn about *Pop Goes the Weasel* –
It had to do with silk worms. The silk
industry only produced one dress
but the song lives on.

IV
Sorrels, Weeds, Cohens –
These are the owners of
The Sorrel Weed House
Somehow the Jews don't get
to have their name on the building.

V
They avoided exterior door taxes
by making the windows large
and walk-throughable.

VI
The men's parlor was decorated with angels
and had a view of Madison Square.
The women's parlor overlooked the chickens.

VII
Pineapple on fence *welcome*.
Pineapple on mantle *time to go.*

Private Residence

We walk by a *private residence* sign.
I want to knock in the door and
ask if I can have a tour. If they say
it's a a private residence, I'll say
I know but it doesn't say you
don't give tours.

Wine Hour

I
While I drink wine at the hotel's wine hour
I take care of all of Addie's needs by
telling her to download a plant identification app
and sending her off to let me know what
tree that is.

II
Now I wonder what else I can identify
with apps on my phone. I point the camera
at the bruise on Addie's leg to see what
it can tell me.

III
The two cups of wine
at the wine hour
at the hotel
have made me
appreciate
the hotel
all the more.

Fourth of July on the Savannah River

It's not my first river
or my first Fourth of July
or my first combination of the two.

We're an hour early because
you never know with crowds
and tall people.

Addie reminds me fireworks
happen in the sky and no one
is as tall as that.

We try to remember
all the cities where we've
experienced this day.

Boston, of course, Paris
which was a non-event for the French.
A couple of northeastern cities

maybe Hartford or somewhere
in New England. Once in
Allentown. This day happens

wherever you are in the world
whether or not I am wearing my
American flag underwear.

Less than an hour now –
The police on their river boats
are regulating civilians who

happen to paddle by.
No one wants the casualties
of another revolution.

We have our place.
The sky is well within view.
Soon it will explode.

On The River

I
A large man and his partner
move to occupy the space next to us.
I start to feel a little claustrophobic
and imagine what if he had asked
If it was okay if he stood there.
It is literally the day of "it's a free country"
is what I would have told him.

II
One thing's for sure –
with all this picture taking
and poetry writing and
text messaging, this is
definitely the night my phone
goes in the Savannah River.

III
Now Addie is worried that her bag
or herself will fall into the river and
I don't see any easy place to climb out
so this may involve swimming
to South Carolina.

IV
At one point,
a few big fireworks
followed by a small one.
Nice job little guy!

V
Someone's flying a drone at eye level
over the river. If I were the boat police
I would arrest that drone.

July 4, 2022

The American gun parade
      has come to Chicago.
The American gun parade
      takes no day off.
The American gun parade
      reminds us nowhere is safe
The American gun parade
      took six more today.
The American gun parade
      left overturned lawn chairs
      in the street.
The American gun parade
      is the jazz of terrorism
      homegrown
      truly ours.

Savannah
Day 2

Checking In

We're going to visit the third oldest
synagogue in America, today

because we just can't turn it off.
That is, if they answer the phone

and tell us we can come.
You never know with these things.

**Figs
Jews
Alcohol
Dinner
Ghosts**

This is
our plan
for today.

Jewcautionary Measures

I put on a nice shirt to
visit the Jews. That and
my proof of vaccination
and they should
let me right in.

Incomplete Instructions

Addie's having caffeine this morning
which is unusual so she tells me to
hang on to my hat, but my hat is
in her bag so I'm not sure how this
is going to work out.

Donuts for Mylan

Mylan, which is the name of a woman
in Chicago whose first name is Rachel
but by law she is referred to as *Mylan*,
says there is a need for coffee and donuts
so with all the powers available to me
here in the state of Georgia, I make it so
coffee and donuts are sent to her.
When Mylan says *donuts*.
one doesn't hesitate.

DF for RW

A couple of phrases I came across that I'm not going to explain for the great acronym user from the great acronym interpreter:

Dookey Freebase
Dildo Fiddle

Congregation Mikveh Israel

I
Photos are okay
but not in the museum
where the ghost
of Debbie Friedman shops

II
Map pins on US
and world maps
tell us who else
has been here.

III
I answer the docent's question
correctly. *Spanish Inquisition.*
I'm a genius on this tour.

IV
Valuables sewn into their clothing –
They escaped from Portugal to London.
Hosted by Bevis Marx Synagogue in London,
they eventually sailed (for five months)
to the new colony of Georgia
where Oglethorpe saw there were
no lawyers amongst the Jews and
he let them in.

V
Rhoda's husband is buried
in the same cemetery as Oglethorpe –
Bonaventure Cemetery.

VI
Mi Chamocha – the oldest version
I've ever heard plays on a *lovely audio*.
We've been singing for our freedom
as long as anyone in town.

VII
This is the first place instrumental music
was played in a synagogue. In this room.

VIII
This sanctuary is beautiful
but I would so rearrange the chairs
before doing anything in here.

IX
This has always been a place
of mixed gender seating.

X
A woman comes in to check
the names on the memorial plaques
on the walls. Shabbes is coming
and the list has to be accurate
for the Rabbi. This is not just history
It is *living* Judaism.

XI
They know so little
about the mystery window
in the sanctuary.

XII
The chanukiah that came over on the boat
looks like a hell of a thing to have to sew
into your skirt to sneak out of Portugal.

XIII
The old bris kit
is not the same thing
as brisket.

XIV
Nunez's great great grandson
bought Monticello from
Thomas Jefferson.

XV
A marriage contract was
found rolled up in a cabinet
in the womens bathroom.
It's not a good sign for how the
marriage fared.

XVI
The first Girl Scout meeting
was held in this building and
the first Girl Scout cookies
we're from Gottlieb's bakery
They're still kosher today.

XVII
Rhoda has been working the latke booth
at the Jewish food festival for years.
That's definitely the line I would be standing in.

XVIII
Rhoda's husband was named *Stephen*.
They broke the mold, she says.
May his name forever be a blessing.

XIX
The portraits of previous rabbis
starting from 1873 get more and
more modern until 1986 when
Rabbi Ostrich brings the beard back
with a vengeance.

Post-Everything Fetish

The cemetery on Punch Bowl Crater is full.
So you cannot be buried there, unless you have
a loved one already there, in which case you
have the option to be buried on top of them
if that's your thing.

Like a

Addie wants to know
If there are any china shops
on Bull Street.

At Forsyth Park

I
Instead of a swimming pool
jets of water shoot out of the ground
for children to frolic in (no dogs allowed).
In Southern California this is known as
broken sprinklers and there would be
a hefty fine.

II
The kids on the swings
are in desperate need of
someone to push them.
The kids today and their
lack of swing set training.

III
A confederate squirrel
eats confederate nuts
in front of the confederate memorial
to the confederate dead
1861 to 1865.

Opinions

An open air tour trolley rolls by
and we overhear the guide say

*this is the most beautiful residential
street in the world.*

That's a subjective statement
I yell towards them and feel

really good about what
I've accomplished here.

Back at Gallery Espresso

We stop for a third time at
Gallery Espresso thanks to
Fritz bringing us here for their
fine bathrooms and delicious treats.
This is our place now.

Prohibition Museum

I
The pioneers called their spirits
good creature of God.

II
You don't get to drink
until the end of the Prohibition Museum
which keeps people from interacting
with the exhibits in an unintended manner.
(People besides me, I should clarify.)

III
In 1808 Georgia became the
eighth state to go dry.
It's not the kind of thing
you want to be first to.

IV
Wets versus Dries –
An expression
long gone.

V
A sign says *please do not*
spit on the stairs or floor
I always appreciate
specific guidelines.

VI
It was not illegal
to drink alcohol
during prohibition –
Just sell it.

VII
Breweries survived by making other products
Coors Malted Milk
Stroh's Pure Malt Syrup
Yeungling Ice Cream
and *Bud Frozen Egg Products*
are a few I did not make up.

VIII
Does anyone really believe it is the function
of government to regulate the habits and
appetites of the people rather than provide
them with jobs? ~Danish times

IX
You could buy a ticket to see a "Blind Pig"
which included a complimentary drink at the end.

X
Because of the sacramental circumvention
allowing the sale of wine for religious purposes
suspect rabbis such as Rabbi O'Leary and
Rabbi McDonough were ordained.

XI
Pretzel flasks filled with liquor.
That's all – Pretzel flasks filled
with liquor.

XII
The father and mother of the Ku Klux Klan
is the anti-saloon league. ~Clarence Darrow

Everything bad starts with those guys.

XIII
During prohibition it was said tailors would ask
what size pockets they wanted? Pints or quarts?
~Will Rogers

XIV
The girls simply won't go out with the boys
who haven't got flasks to offer.
~Police chief, Topeka, Kansas

XV
We head into the speakeasy
and they mix a *Brown Derby* for me.
Bourbon, grapefruit and honey.

It reminds Addie of beer
because of the grapefruit.
This drink is nice and I'm wondering

if I should leave all today's subsequent typos
as they are to legitimize the experience.
In the next room prohibition is over

and we can already hear the *soundtrack of joys.*
I didn't come to alcohol until I was 33
so I've never chugged a beer

unlike the medical students where
Addie went to college.
They could really drink she says.

My prohibition ended years ago
and it's all about the artistry now.
What makes this different than that?

Why is older better?
What is it that I like most between my lips,
on my tongue, and down my throat?

Thanks to the repeal of the
Eighteenth Amendment, I have
the rest of my life to find out.

XVI
We both realize the restaurant we were at last night
with the insanely well stocked bar was called *Repeal*.
It's all coming together.

XVII
Prohibition ended in 1933
Happy days are beer again.

XVIII
*Once, during prohibition, I was forced to live
on nothing but food and water.*
~ WC Fields

XIX
Prohibition was the *noble experiment*.
I'd say it failed but the Supreme Court is
offering so many other experiments lately
It feels like the *good* old days.

XX
We walk out the entrance backwards
and I ask if we can get our money back.
She laughs but doesn't say *yes*.

It's Like North Versus South

We see a dog with the
doggiest dog face I've ever seen.
A man asks if we are dog people
we tell him we have cats and
he tells us to enjoy our weekend
even though it's Tuesday.

The Savannah tap room says

You can't drink all day if you
don't start in the morning.
That's why they open at 11.

Ghost Tour

I
The guide asks if we have bug spray
I assure her being eaten alive by bugs
is part of the tour.

II
The lights in Oglethorpe Square are not on
despite Addie's best clapping.

III
The locusts haunt us
every few minutes in
Oglethorpe Square.

IV
An empty *Ghosts and Gravestones* trolly
rolls by.

Or is it?

V
Ashley instructs us to not get hit by a car
or else we're obligated to come back and
haunt the tour which Addie feels would be
a win-win.

VI
Ashley got married in a cemetery
so that's pretty legit.

VII
At night Savannah is so quiet
it sounds like screaming.

VIII
Alice Riley, dressed in black,
wanders around Oglethorpe Square
asking *where is my baby, where is my baby?*

IX
Spanish moss doesn't grow
where innocent blood was shed.

X
The old jail is now a CVS
that closes at 10 pm
when things start flying
off shelves.

XI
700 spots tonight –
We'll be walking
on bodies.

XII
Don't ever die in Savannah.

XIII
Little Sheftal died of acorn poisoning.
Addie puts a rock on his marker
as is our way.

XIV
If we're staying in a hotel
in the historic district
then it's definitely haunted.
One of the hotels, according to Ashley,
is *super haunted.*

XV
In Foley House, Walter,
or *Wally*, was stuck between
the walls for years.

XVI
People in Savannah don't take out walls
as they don't want to find bodies.

XVII
Marshall House Hotel was a union hospital
during the coldest winter. They couldn't bury
amputated limbs in the ground and found them
in 1999 during renovations when the floorboards
were pulled up.

XVIII
Performing surgery –
The drunk operated on
the party goers watching
the performance.
The more blood on the surgeon's
apron, the more credential he had.

XIX
Much of the ghost tour
and its stories take place
on Bull Street.

XX
She tells us a common
local paint color is called *haint* blue.
I tell her no it *haint*.

XXI
Once you see your first ghost
the appropriate response from the locals
is *welcome to Savannah!*

XXII
Dead ringer
Saved by the bell –
Two phrases which
came from yellow fever.
People in comas, not dead
but entombed, fingers tied to
a string, attached to a bell.
If they got better from death
they'd ring the bell
like a *dead ringer*, and
if they were lucky, the *night shift*
would save them, *by the bell.*

Midnight in My Mouth
of Good and Evil

Savannah is where *Midnight in the Garden of Good and Evil* is set.
So, late one night, by Addie's standards, when she realizes
it's almost midnight, and says *it's already midnight*
there was no more perfect time or place for me to say
in the garden of good and evil, which I did, and it was,
in fact, perfect.

A Haunted Poem

Oooh...oooh...ooooh!
Ooooooooooooooooooh!
Welcome to Savannah!

Goodnight Savannah

We've spent a lot of Savannah
walking up and down Bull Street.

Many of its squares, built upon
the dead of one war of another

lay upon its path. We can't believe
this is only the second full day

of our vacation. The heat and
especially the water in the air

are taking it out of us.
All of it.

This hasn't stopped the work emails
from coming in, but it's not fair

to any of us to mention that.
I wonder how many pages

are left to write words on?
I wonder if the humidity will

follow us to the island tomorrow.
I wonder if, by the time we hit Charleston

this will feel like a million miles ago.
I'm getting ahead of myself when

all I should be worried about is
morning lavender coffee

and even before that
eyes wide shut.

Savannah

Day 3

This Morning

I think I inhaled a healthy portion
of spray on sunscreen.

Good morning Savannah!
My insides are protected

from whatever you're
sending us today.

At Collins Quarter

They bring us a lot of food.
More than I'd usually eat —
Large slices of Bananas Foster

French Toast, a side of bacon
that magically turned into hash browns
after I identified myself and my diet.

I ask Addie if I should eat more
in case we get shipwrecked today
She says if we get shipwrecked

I'm going to need to learn to eat crab.
I say *you don't think it will be one of those
islands with lots of tropical fruits.*

She says *we're not in the tropics.*
I say *you don't think it'll be one of those
islands that the conquistadors brought over*

lots of fruit from the tropics?
She pauses, and then says
eat as much as you want.

Fitzroy at Collins Quarter

whose name may not be *Fitzroy*
but it's what it says on his shirt
is the friendliest man in Savannah.
He does everything. He seated us,
took our order, brought our food
cleaned a nearby table, and then
took up residence at a nearby wall
to monitor the room like staff
in a Tudor house. It turns out
his name is *Sidney* which was also
the name of our waitress from last night
so that's kind of like our thing.

On A Trolley

I
If I were to tell you
I'm on an air conditioned trolly
would you believe me?

II
Even the words
Stand Behind the White Line
make me uncomfortable.
They could have picked
any other color.

III
There's a hole in Addie's
brand new shirt, and not
in any of the good places.
First wearing. Kohl's —
be prepared for a visit.

The Tybee Island Dolphin Tour

I
Our tour guide is Dennis.
He says to never get a tour guide talking
as you'll never get him to stop.

He wants to know, at the very beginning,
if we're already a big happy family.
There is an indifferent response from the crowd
Like any family.

Let's do this thing he says
before driving our air conditioned trolley
out of Savannah.

II
We leave the historic district
the largest in the United States.
I see my first strip mall for days.
Sometimes I forget I'm in America.

III
We drive over a big bump.
We throw that party in for free
Dennis tells us.

IV
He tells us we're driving through
the modern part of Savannah and
all I can see is marshland.
I like what they haven't done
with the place.

V
The first golf game in America
was played here in the late 1700s
which I'm sure would interest my
father in law. Hi Bernie, in case
you're reading this.

VI
Dennis tells us he still has
a little bit of a Evil Knievel
in him as we approach
the draw bridge in case
it starts to open.

VII
After the bridge we have
left the mainland and are
officially on an island.

VIII
Oakland Island didn't last
very long and now we're on
Whitemarsh Island which
is pronounced *Whitemarsh*
and not *Whitemarsh*.

IX
We keep crossing bridges.
I have no idea what island
I'm on any more.

X
The Savannah River empties out
into the Atlantic Ocean.
The Crab Shack is minutes away.
I'm looking forward to the nearby
alligators more so than the seafood.

XI
At the Crab Shack

In a perfect windstorm
at The Crab Shack
a menu lifts up off the table
and presses against Addie's face.
I laugh heartily like I never do
and apologize for doing so
at Addie's misfortune but my
rare hearty laugh is really
all she wanted.

XII
Still at the Crab Shack

The Crab Shack is *where*
the elite go to eat in their bare feet.
We have shoes on in appropriate
deference to our station in this
part of the world.

To say it is not a Mecca for vegetarians
is to say alligators have sharp teeth.
The amount of time they have allotted
for this stop will give us sufficient time
to turn into Florida skeletons.
I bet a lot of vegetarian's skeletons
have been permanently stored in
The Crab Shack floorboards.

I dare Addie to ask
if they have gluten free saltines.
She politely declines.

You did a fine job on this iced tea
I tell the bartender just to make conversation.

XIII
Yes, we are still at The Crab Shack

as rigor mortus kicks in
and the wind blows
and regimes change
and alligators age
and the bartender heads away
to get more ice.

I dare Addie again
to ask the bartender
if they have gluten free saltines.
I know I already said that.
We've just been here so long
I've run out of things to say.

The bartender for no particular reason
and to no one in particular says
Whatchu talkin 'bout Willis.

I hear what sounds like the tuba
from a New Orleans brass band
and I'm about to get into it but
then realize it's just an ongoing
series of people's chairs rubbing
against The Crab Shack floors.
Rascal's Got Fire
Rascal's Got Fire

XIV
Did I Mention We're Still at The Crab Shack?

The Crab Shack manager slash bartender
slash nice person gives us the iced tea for free
which makes it all worthwhile.

Despite the fact that we had enough time
to establish a new civilization during our
The Crab Shack stop, a few people still
manage to be late back to the trolley.

The Crab Shack has been on Tybee Island
for 50 or 60 years which is about
the same amount of time we've been
waiting to get back on the tour bus.

XV
We have to wait another fifteen minutes
once we get to *Captain Derek's Dolphin Adventure.*
Time enough for Addie to notice there's a hole in my shorts
right where my butt is. I bought these a hundred years ago
so there's no trip to Kohl's in my immediate future.

XVI
Addie and I share
Airplane nuts at the picnic table.
Mostly almonds.

XVII
Dolphin Magic

I was on a boat –
Dolphin Magic

It was longer than 27 feet
and had a bathroom, so,
technically, it was a yacht.

I was on a yacht
on the Atlantic Ocean
Dolphin Magic.

I was expecting a
chatty Flipper.
Instead I got a few fins
and an occasional nose.

The guide, Connor,
told us *the Pacific Ocean is mean.*
I apologized.

XVIII
Tybee Island Light House

Six platforms
One hundred seventy-seven steps –
Our feet touched every one.
Our lips pressed against
each other at every level.

XIX
Next stop the beach
North shore. We're asked to
stay out of the sand dunes
so as not to disturb the turtles.

XX
We take
a few minutes
at the gazebo.

XXI
I might have a concussion
from hitting my head on
something in the lighthouse.
If my poems got even more
nonsensical, you'll know why.

XXII
An island
dolphins and
all the way up
a lighthouse –
This is a
win win win
for a Lupert vacation.

XXIII
I ask Addie if she knows
if there's a sink in the men's bathroom.
The conversation doesn't go very far.

XXIV
Addie wants to
give me a concussion test
so she moves her finger around
and asks me to follow it.
I would follow that finger anywhere.

Then she asks me if I know what day it is.
It turns out neither of us knew what day it was
so it was a terrible test to administer.

XXV
I just remember that on the boat
Connor gave us detailed statistics
about how we would probably not
get eaten by a shark if we went into
the Atlantic Ocean. Jaws is one of the
first movies I ever saw, and the statistics
I learned from that film do not back up
what Connor told us.

XXVI
We leave Tybee Island the same way we came –
On a blue bus shaped like a trolly.
That's right folks, the trolley was a bus
this whole time. And what have we learned here?
Cue the sentimental music.
(Ideally the M.A.S.H. end credits music.)

XXVII
Dennis says the question of the day is
How long does it take to build a bridge
over the Wilmington River?
We may never know is the answer
as we drive by a project that has been going on
since, possibly, the Civil War.

One For the History Books

Savannah is a city obscenely rich with history.
From Oglethorpe to the Revolutionary War to
the Civil War to the founding of the Girl Scouts
to, possibly, where ghosts were invented.

Savannah is an egregiously beautiful city.
The many public squares (despite who is
buried under them), the river, the trees,
my God the live oaks are everything.

Savannah is a city of democrats surrounded
by alligators, with a Confederate monument
smack-dab in the middle of the park. Do you
tear those things down or leave them to remember?

Savannah is a city of art and smiles.
Of biscuits and *y'all,* of Bull Street running
through everything and Broughton Street
torn up to remind us there's always more to do.

We'd like to do more, to never leave (if they'd
consider turning off the water in the air.)
To always came back, to walk these streets again.
To see what history does next.

From
Savannah to
Charleston

Breakfast

I
We almost ate at the place where there are
flat tops at every table and you make your
own pancakes but we didn't because
what the hell are we paying these people for?

II
They have a coffee grinder so big
at *Blends Coffee*, it has its own ZIP Code.

Thank You Savannahians!

I'm wearing my *Fifteen Years Married* t-shirt despite the fact that it is not our anniversary and we've been married for eighteen years. It's causing a lot of confusion among the local congratulators but it's just a really comfortable t-shirt.

Savannah house doors are red

if the owner has paid off their mortgage.
At least in the 18 and 1900s.
Addie wants that, but we'll have to
check with the HOA first
in another thirty years.

At Pelindaba Lavender

I
They advertise the *complete lavender experience*.
Little do they know the lengths they'll need to go through
to create *my* complete lavender experience.

II
When we walk in, I once again
prove I'm the most clever boy in Savannah
when I ask them *has anyone ever told you
it smells like lavender in here?*

III
Overheard in the lavender store –
a customer telling the story of how
someone they knew got malaria
and then typhus. This *is* the
complete lavender experience!

IV
*Comfortable shirt
comfortable marriage*
The owner tells us.

Pre-Nostalgic

Have you ever had the thought
when you walked out of a building
that it might be the last time you
ever were going to be in that building?
It happens a lot on vacation
and it's very sad.

Uber

I
Car smells like cigarettes –
Not the last scent of Savannah
we wanted.

This guy could use the
complete lavender experience.

II
The Historic District
is one twenty-fifth of Savannah.
We see a good deal of the
other twenty-four on the way to
Budget Rental Car.

III
His GPS speaker sounds
as friendly as he does.
At least *she's* making conversation.

IV
We drive by the Savannah Mortgage Globe
which is a sign from God since we're going to
have dinner tonight in Charleston with our
mortgage broker from eighteen years ago.

On The Road Again

I

The Luperts have arrived in Charleston
is what I'll message my friends when we
actually get there, but we just left Savannah
and have another couple of hours on the road
so hang on to your hats y'all!

II

We cross the Coosawhatchie River
and now I know for sure my next goldfish
will be named *Coosawhatchie.*

III

A billboard advertises *Potty Like a Rockstar.*
Another item for the bucket list.

IV

We drive by the Frampton Plantation.
I had no idea he was that old and I wonder
if this is where he pottied like a rock star

Uber

I
The Road out of Savannah is the Charleston Highway.
As you get closer to Charleston it becomes the
Savannah Highway. *Sister cities* Moe tells us
on the way to the hotel. *These two cities*
been kissing cousins since my grandpappy
made moonshine in the Blue Ridge Mountains
I tell him.

II
I don't have the heart to tell him in Savannah
they told me Charleston was their rival.

III
On first glance Charleston
is not as beautiful as Savannah
But our driver may be taking
the back roads.

They're Made of People

While on an impromptu walking tour of all of downtown Charleston
we arrive at the Charleston Pier where we find average citizens
leaning over the fence to watch dolphins do what dolphins do.
A young boy leans down to an even younger boy and asks
Do you know what dolphins eat? The younger boy looks up
with the widest and most curious eyes and the older younger boy
says *babies*. That conversation is everything we know about
the relationship between these two young boys.

Roger and Lydia

We eat dinner with our former and first mortgage broker,
Roger and his wife, Lydia, who moved to Charleston

from Los Angeles on a whim. They had never been here,
bought a house sight-unseen. *How bad could it be*

they thought since it showed up so high on all the internet lists.
They feed us at the best restaurant. They dessert us too.

Then we walk the city, Roger taking the lead while I ask
incessant questions about what streets cross what other streets.

I like to know the lay of the land and he appreciates that.
It could be a male thing and we are both males, while

Addie and Lydia converse a small handful of steps behind us.
These are people who live their life deliberately, a reminder

permanently around Roger's wrist says to do so.
Roger made it so I could live in a house for the first time ever.

That was eighteen years ago and he has turned from a
mortgage broker into a person. I suspect he was always

a person, but often the people we simply transact with
never rise beyond the transactions in our hearts and minds.

Well, thanks to dinner, and conversation, and miles on our
tired feet, on cobblestones brought over on a ship in the

seventeenth century, we have two new people in our lives.
Welcome aboard, friends.

Charleston

Day 1

Goodbye Charleston

Okay so day one in Charleston
actually involves leaving Charleston
on a day trip to the Boone Hall Plantation.
Can someone email me a concise history
of Charleston so I can have the much needed
context to wander around this city later tonight?

Turn Back a Page to Understand

Look at how the lines of that last poem
get further and further out to the right like
I'm building a stairway, except for line four
which indicates no-one vetted the plans
properly.

P.S. Why is *properly* on it's own line above?
This is getting ridiculous.

This morning

I am not wearing a shirt
that is indicating anything except
the color blue so no one will assume
it is any particular anniversary allowing
only our extreme collective cuteness to
light the way from Charleston all the way
to the Boone Hall Plantation.

Not 5 7 5

By special request
there will be nothing in this book
about *dream peeing*.

Our Crops Our Saved!

I'm coming in too hot and fast
(or is it hot and heavy
or is it dream peeing)
with my thick southern
plantation owner accent
for anyone's comfort level.

On The Way To Boone Hall

I
The visitor center used to be a train station.
The train used to go up to twenty-five miles per hour
which the local paper described as
annihilating time and space.
Our driver is not convinced we
will achieve the annihilation of time and space
on our way to Boone Hall.

II
The Charleston Welcome Gate
is closed and locked for some reason.

III
We shall overcome
came from *we will overcome*
came from a cigar factory
came from a cotton gin.
An earthquake was involved.

IV
There are fancier names for
everything in Charleston.

Porches are *piazzas*
Swamps are *marshes*
Roaches are *palmetto bugs*
Earthquakes are *land massages*
Pickles are *finely spiced cucumbers*
Houses are *living wall establishments*
Farms are *plantations*
Civil Wars are *gentlemen's points of contention*
Parrots are *avian communications specialists*
Some of these I made up.

V
Addie says *fish*.
Imagine if you taught a frog
to say the word *fish*.
That's what it sounded like.
I taught her how to do this in Brugges
a hundred years ago and we've
been laughing about it ever since.

VI
We're on the King's Highway on which
it used to take three months to travel
from Boston to Charleston.

VII
Shawn tells us Savannah
is the drunk sister of Charleston.

VIII
We drive by eagles nests.
I tell Addie *we should get an eagle.*
That's your answer for everything
she says.

At Boone Hall Plantation

I
You paint your porch ceiling haint blue
to keep the evil spirits and the birds away.
One color blind bird didn't get the memo.

II
It's a large tour inside the house.
No photos allowed so you'll
just have to trust me.

III
Book wire covers the book shelves
instead of glass to prevent moisture.
When chicken wire is brought inside
it is called *book wire*.

IV
The doors in the house are wide
to accommodate the five foot wide
skirts on the four foot eleven ladies.

V
They didn't have selfies back then
so the furniture artists would just
carve themselves into the wood.

VI
Breakfast was a *come and go* thing.
Lunch was munchies for the hunters.
Dinner was three hours in this room.
But only if you were over thirteen years old.

VII
I'll take my scones in the breezeway
is the new fancy voice *this is where*
we shall dine tonight.

VIII
The state bird is the mosquito.

IX
The doorway to Mister Stone's man cave
was much too narrow for the ladies.

X
They've been growing crops here
nonstop since 1681.

XI
The plantation borders a housing development
and Angus is happy to turn off his mic as
we drive through the quiet zone.

XII
Boone Hall lost seventy percent of
its pecan trees during Hurricane Hugo.

XIII
How many deer we have?
A gozillion, Angus says.

XIV
We see an empty field where a corn maze will grow.
Now is the easiest time to solve a corn maze.

XV
Electric fence
protects the cash crop –
Cantaloupe.

XVI
They grow peaches here
to honor the original owners.

XVII
They're experimenting with hemp.

XVIII
Thomas Boone planted oaks
to mature for the people
yet to come.

XIX
After the tractor tour
I book it to the Gullah Theater
to get in my fast steps and
wear down my body to
be able to fully weep
during the presentation.

XX
The Gullah tour starts late because
the Gullah lady left her instrument
elsewhere on the plantation and needs
to drive to go get it.

XXI
Jump the broom –
They weren't allowed to get married
so they *jumped the broom.*

Black eyed peas –
If less were on the ground,
eyes were watching you.
Don't take that path.

Hush puppies –
They fed these to the dogs
to make them sleepy and keep them quiet.

XXII
I done done what
I had to do.

XXIII
Children are asked to
not touch the butterflies.
Adults can go full-on
butterfly molest
apparently.

Another Weather Report From Addie

I'm worried about the weather in Asheville
because everyone says it's cooler there but
that's just relative to here and Addie assures me
it will not be bumblefuck degrees there.

Free Bus

We get on a free bus to take us
from the Visitors Center to the dungeon.
Actually waitaminute, what the hell
are we doing here?

On the Streets

I
There's a store on King Street
called *Collard Greens* which only sells clothing.

I assume their memo is en-route.

II
I kiss Addie at the intersection of
King and Queen streets for reasons
I shouldn't have to explain to any of you.

Provost Dungeon

I
The guide offers to extend the tour from
thirty-nine to ninety minutes if we'd like.

He says if the insurance on our phones is paid up
we're welcome to take a picture of him.

He is not bothered by movement
during the presentation which will soon
lead to my fabulous dungeon jig of freedom.

A little girl asks if there are any ghosts
in the dungeon. The guide says he hasn't
seen any but it's the perfect time for me to make
my *ooooh...oooooh* noises.

Charleston is at least two and a half blocks
larger into the bay thanks to the ballast rocks
emptied into the harbor.

II
Painting Observations

General Francis Marion
was born at Goatfield Plantation.

General Andrew Pickens
had a long long head.

The battle of Cowpens
is something that existed.

The real Lafayette didn't rap
but the people loved him anyway.

III
I'm standing in the room
where the constitution was ratified.
Ratified means approved
I approve.

IV
In 1860 the four million American slaves
were conservatively valued at
three billion dollars.

V
One hundred fifty men,
women and children who
came here in April of 1670,
began to impose European order
on what looked like a wilderness.
The ship – Carolina.

Back on the Street

I
An old store called *Read and Read* is closed.
Nobody reads and reads anymore.

II
A sign by St. Phillip's church
says *the only ghost at Phillips
is the Holy Ghost* which I guess
will save us a lot of money
on the local ghost tours that
walk by this location.

Burping With Wine and Cheese

I

After burping during the wine and cheese hour
at the French Quarter Inn, a man at the next table says
hell yeah and I like to assume he was
super impressed with what I just did.

Actually Addie burped first and mine came
soon after which prompted me to announce
gather round, the Luperts have begun
to the assembled wine drinkers and cheese eaters.

This, in turn, prompted Addie to try to find
Debbie Friedman's song *Gather Round*
which I thought was a different song
and she tapped the table when I started to
sing that one and say *you're going to
get that song out of my head.*

II

I don't know why they served the
Cabernet cold but I've been here long
enough that it has transformed to
an acceptable temperature.

III

We've had enough wine
that Addie and I are now
running through all the songs
we know about frogs.

IV

I'm confusing all the frog songs
and I don't know which one has a frog
and which one has a hole.

In Our Hotel Room

When the air condition turns off
the light in the middle of the room
lights up like lightning.

This causes no great concern
because the lightning we've been
seeing outside

has yet to cause me any problems
so why would a much smaller version
located in this room be an issue?

Good Night Charleston

It turns out Charleston is rich with history too.
This peninsula, expanded by the waste of ships
where *King* and *Queen* intersect
where revolutions turned over and over
where Civil Wars started
where, through it all, a building selling liquor
has been doing so since 1686
where the old and new commingle on restaurant menus
where cobblestones make everyone's feet uncomfortable
where there is so much to do and so little time to do it in
where everything to write, was written before.
Two eagle's nests on the top of palm trees
Artists on the street every day
I hardly know these streets –
These hidden alleys.
There are ghosts here too.
Let them be.

Charleston

Day 2

Good Morning Charleston

This morning I only have berries for breakfast
as we're going on a culinary walking tour
and I want my stomach to be as available
as possible for all the bounty that's coming its way.
If you're painting a picture, please
add in a small croissant (which people
in America rarely pronounce correctly)
as the berry plate was a little empty
for my liking. As long as you're still
painting, Addie just brought back a peach,
sliced it up and now that's joining the party.
I hope it's a slow walking tour and they've
taken into consideration that some of us have
just had breakfast, *for heaven's sake.*
Did I mention the coffee at this hotel?
It's better than coffee at *most places.*
Addie just noticed an open lily at
a nearby table and this whole breakfast
is becoming a *still life* situation. You
are the artists. We are the subjects.
We'll be considering this for years.

Supplemental Thought

I packed my own vitamins and supplements
in all the compartments which is something
that Addie usually does and apparently
I'm not as good at counting as every day
it seems there's a different number of
things in the compartments and often
not the number that I actually need.
My body is sighing at this situation and
resolved to deal with my lackadaisical
attention to detail and hopes it can
pull its resources together for another week
when it arrives home and it's easy to
remember what to do and when.

Syllables

The ballad of
the sweet coffee mug licker
plays on.

Hello Reader

Is this your first time reading
a Rick Lupert travel poetry book
or have you had this experience before?
We'd appreciate a review
on Amazon or TripAdvisor or Yelp
or write it on a public bathroom stall
beginning with the words *for a good time read*.
Thank you for taking my words
into your eyes.

She Is

Addie shoos away a bug with
a pleasant *no thanks* and I
imagine that bug going back
to its friends and saying
*that's the nicest lady I ever
tried to infest.*

Culinary Walking Tour
Slave Market
Distillery

If today was a sandwich
the slave market would be
the protein.

P.S. It would have been more common
to say *meat* instead of *protein* but
I'm a vegetarian and trying to be
true to my voice.

Culinary Walking Tour

I
Benne wafer
Sweet, Sesame
From Africa

II
The Charleston Crab Shack

Mimi seats Addie and I across from each other
So the vegetarians can gaze into each other's eyes
while everyone else eats crab.

Frogmore Stew is low country boil.

Charleston has been social
since 1679 when the British
landed with boatfuls of ale.

The Spanish brought the pigs.
We cannot leave any shrimp behind.

Do you just watch us eat, Addie asks
I talk Mimi says.

The first American structure
meant to be a theater
is here in Charleston.

They got the king's
DNA here.

Rice was the money crop.
It died at the Civil War.

Indigo died at the revolution.
The third cash crop was cotton.

The enslaved were targeted for their knowledge.
The Senegalese and Sierra Leon knew rice.

III
Oyster House

Not sure what I'll eat here
but at least it begins with *Oy*.

Thomas Ravenal
the spoiled Ravenel
had to resign as state treasurer
because he got caught
distributing cocaine
He was the youngest of six
They named the bridge
after his daddy.

I'm instructed to watch
One episode of *Southern Charm*
to understand this part
of the conversation.

Corn, grits, polenta, corn meal –
The natives gave it to us.

These hush puppies with praline butter
are worth the price of admission.

I trade Addie half a hush puppy
for my asparagus.

Shrimp and grits used to be simpler –
Salt and pepper and shrimp and grits.
But about forty-nine years ago
the chefs became *artists*.

I head to the bathroom and
miss some of the narration
and when I come out she's
talking about cocaine so
I'm not sure what happened to
this food tour while I was away.

Pimento cheese came from New York
But Mimi says *they didn't do it right*
So it became a *Southern thing.*

Grated cheddar, a dash of salt
pimentos and Duke's Mayo –
Hellman's is a typo.
Miracle Whip is blasphemy.
This has been a brief aside
about pimento cheese
and the history of mayonnaise.

If you're going to eat pimento cheese
don't put it in a piece celery –
That just negates the whole thing.

I eat pimento cheese on a Saltine
so as to legitimize the whole experience.

She Crab Soup is the signature dish
It's the Lysistrata of appetizers.

The food here is assimilated –
Not like Little Italy or Chinatown.
The base of all of it is the pig.

This is the least Kosher conversation
I've ever had.

Fine southern cuisine is just
prettied up *Geechee* and *Gullah.*

The most tolerant place is built
on the back of slavery.

Free blacks had to pay a tax every year.
Most free blacks owned slaves.

They would purchase their relatives if they could.
It was safer to be owned by a relative than to be a free black.
The blacks had the biggest influence on the cuisine.

In 1800 Charleston had the largest Jewish community
in the United States.

The Scots brought the worst recipe –
Crab soup. Just crab and water.
No one in the British isles seasoned their food.

Gullah ladies don't fill and empty the dish washer
They *dress* and *undress* the dishwasher.

Gullah is a dying language because
early childhood educators tell the kids
that's not proper English.

The August 31, 1886 earthquake number keeps going down
with every tour guide
7.5
7.4
7.3 Mimi tells us.
Soon it will be *someone bumped into a building*
and the exaggeration began.
Anyway, the buildings are bolted together
just in case.

IV
Poogan's Smokehouse

Bring me a live pig
We'll give it a name
and bring it home.

Yard babies!

A *great fire* is one
that takes out three hundred or more buildings.
Charleston had five great fires.

Barbecue came from
Barbados's to the Carolinas to
the mouths of everyone
in America.

A not so brief aside is taken
to cover the story of the Murdaugh family
Invoking murder, dogs and a boat crash.
Just good old boys
Never meaning no harm.

V
Carmella's Dessert Bar

Addie points out the strawberry shortcake
which I observe is kind of tall for a shortcake.

Mimi's real name is Amelia Whaley.

She's from here.
Way from here.

At the Slave Mart Museum

I
Shackles
The middle passage
Labor
Branding
Runaway
Reward
Labor
Lincoln
Emancipation
War
Death
Freedom

II
My master whipped my gran-mammy with a leather strap...
whipped her like he didn't have no soul to save.
~Hector Smith, ex-slave, South Carolina

III
The first person sold here
was twenty year old Lucinda –
1856.

The last person sold here
walked through the doors.

The Powder Magazine

I
Mitchell at *The Powder Magazine*
the oldest public building in Charleston
circa 1713, is more than proud to
have us honor him with questions.

II
Addie at The Powder Magazine
is in love with the feather pen they gave her
to do the quiz.

III
Addie is firing digital cannon balls
at digital pirates. Jude would be
so proud.

Three Problems in Charleston

I
Addie *just can't* with the
out of tune church bells.
No, no, no she chants
as each accidental note rings.

II
Toast All Day
is not a bread products
establishment

III
The men's bathroom
at the Mills House Hotel
is right next to the storage room.
I walk in the wrong door and they
keep me on file for
two hundred and fifty years.

Nathaniel Russell House

Your skin has acids and oils she says
but it sounds like *asses and oils.*

Nathaniel Russel bragged he could
make more money selling one slave
than he could selling 65,000 barrels of rum.

Russell's desk was $9000
when it was made in 1808.
I think I'd be okay with a $5000 desk.

It's a cantilever staircase.
I'm more of a *can*ilever guy.

He painted his doors to look like mahogany
because it was more expensive and fashionable
than less expensive, actual mahogany.

I see the room where we will dine tonight.

The plates and silverware are original.
The spoon is giant. They must have had
giant mouths back then.

I think we're on the tour where
everyone else came from afternoon drinking
based on their happiness and verbosity.

The back parlor which we are standing in
was never for guests. The Russels
must be rolling over in their whatever they
are buried in.

The room we entered is called the *hyphen*.
I can't wait to get to the *semicolon*.

They take us up the back staircase
as is our lot in life.

A large open sugar bowl
like in the lesser drawing room
showed they were wealthy and
you could have as much sugar as you want.

Single use pieces of furniture –
Like the small table that held up
the hot water urn.

I can tell Addie is excited about
the tea storage box.

The door surround
was called the
door surround.

Harriett tells us they were able to duplicate the trim
because a rat had stored a piece of it in its nest.
I ask if the descendants of the original rats
still live here and if they were on the confederate
or union side. She says they were probably confederate rats
and adds on we're a lively group.

Old Simon was only worth five dollars
according to a sign in the enslaved persons
quarters. How wrong they were.

We take a picture of Addie at the headless,
butt-full statue.

Three More Charleston Things

I
Addie is concerned she's getting bugs in all her crevices.
She probably doesn't want me to write that down
but here we are.

II
Can you really trust a beef jerky store
that misspells it as *beff* on one of their signs?

III
I feed Addie a piece of chamomile raspberry chocolate
and announce *you have just experienced Rick's
famous chocolate tour! No charge.*

At Church and Union

I
Oh my sweet God of Christ
Please rise for the *Shema*
in this old church turned food place
after wine earlier
and a *Fresno Old Fashioned.*

II
The checks come in copies of
The Art of War by Sun Tzu.
They call it *the grey book*
as no one wants to overtly
remind you about war
while you eat.

We hover for seats at the bar
Where it's every man, woman, and
mammal for themselves.

We sit at the bar next to a standing guy
Who keeps bumping into me and whose name
turns out to be *Rick* which is great because
you can't catch COVID from a guy who
has the same name as you.

We Shall Pizza, Come

Man with green hat and green shirt
standing under Saint Hotel awning
holding pizza box. Light changes.
Man crosses street. I don't know
if I'll ever see this man again
but we head to pizza to
eat in his mouthsteps.

In Kilwin's Dessert Shop

Addie doesn't think there's real turtle
in the turtle cheesecake ice cream.

Goodnight Charleston

Addie is asleep and I am using a dim light
to assemble words I know in a manner that
might serve to give meaning to the day.

According to the clock, it is already a new day
but that hasn't stopped my fingers from
assessing the weight of history.

Nathaniel Russell bragged about the money
he could make from selling a single human.
A building so strong it survived an earthquake

was put up to house human cattle.
We walked through the showroom just like
we might through *Urban Outfitters.*

Another building, the oldest *public* one
in Charleston, existed only to house the powder
used to make guns of every size work.

So much of what we've seen was built
using the hands of people whose descendants
still don't feel free. What a country, America.

We are the divided, the criminal, the forever
red and blue feud. How embarrassing I think
as I turn it off to eat cookie samples

while the rain falls on Charleston.

Charleston
Day 3

By the way –

The water bottles at our hotel are made of aluminum. Does that make them cans, or do I still get to call them bottles?

Biscuits Before War

It's a mad dash to
Callie's Hot Biscuit
for a pickup order
to eat back at the hotel
where they have the
perfect coffee, in time
to take a car, to a boat
to an island with a fort
where the first person
let something fly
out of his weapon
beginning something
bloody and violent
that we still refer to
as *civil*.

What To Do?

We have an awkward amount of time –
too soon to take a car to the place.
We consider walking leisurely
but aren't sure what there is to see
along the way so I ask Addie if
she thinks it might be the biggest
mistake of our lives. She doesn't
have to think long to come up with
a few others higher on the list.

Our New Things

I have a new thing where every time
we contemplate whether to do
something (where to have dinner,
what museum to go to, etc...)
I say this might be the biggest mistake
of our lives. Addie's working on her new
thing too which is adjusting my collar
which makes part of my face move.

Fort Sumter

I
I'd like to report that, once again,
Addie and I are on a boat. A ferry
specifically that will take us to
an Island. It is important to report
and note when one is on an island
just as much so as when one is
on a boat, though there is no
song to commemorate this moment
as much as there is one for when
you are on a boat.

II
An Amish couple gets on the boat.
Or maybe it's just a farmer and his wife
from a hundred years ago.
I'm going to carbon date his beard.

III
I see St. Phillips Church from the boat.
There's our church I tell Addie and she
knows what I mean as I've taken so many
photos of this landmark. I don't think
we're going to lead services there
anytime soon, but, like Dublin's pole,
it marks the center of the city – a landmark
to always let us know where we are.

IV
The rangers in the boat discuss
James Bond and which ones they
feel are important. George Lazenby
doesn't make the list, which is a shame.

V
Clouds cover the sun
which is all I have ever
wanted them to do.

VI
The first shots of the Civil War
which couldn't possibly be what
they called it back then, were fired
from one island to another.

VII
We might see dolphins on this boat ride
which might mean we could have saved
a lot of money on the dolphin specific tour.
We haven't actually seen any yet though
so I will pause before passing judgment.

VIII
The boat leaves at 1:35 which means
we need to be on the boat before 1:35
or else we need to reimagine our lives
as permanent residents of Fort Sumter.

IX
The sandbar is off limits.

X
A house divided against itself cannot stand.
~Abraham Lincoln

XI
George S. James fired the first shot in the civil war.

XII
We see the sword Captain George S. James
was wearing when he ordered the first shot.

XIII
Lincoln ordered seventy-five thousand troops
to *put down* the rebellion.

XIV
Going to the bathroom
on a boat is a Civil War of
precise geometry and prayer.

XV
Based on their beard,
clothing, eye patch, tzitzit,
and intense coughing,
we can't tell if they're
Amish, Jews, pirates, or
super spreaders.

XVI
We do, in fact,
see dolphins.

XVII
I correct a typo
avoiding talking about
the first *shit*
of the Civil War.

XVIII
I will forever
look for dolphins
in the wakes of boats.

XIX
We see
more
dolphins.

XX
Addie is done with history for now
and is ready for arts and culture and
ice cream. We're right by an aquarium
so I wonder if she'd be into *fishtory*.

Not Really Something From This Trip, But I Thought it Up While Here

I went to a dueling piano bar and I was surprised when they used pistols.

King Street In The Rain

I
Cuban coffee
Cafecito
Coming soon

Doughnuts
Closed.

We've come to King Street
at the wrong time.
(Unless we want toast all day.)

II
I wonder how the people
at the Goorin Bros Hat Shop

feel about the Hotel Bennet
lobby sign that says

Gentlemen, please
remove your hats.

III
I forgot to tell you about Addie's standard
check for deodorant in the glove box of the rental car
from a few days ago which has been going on since
the great rental car deodorant discovery of 2014.

IV
The pedestrian event which closes down
this end of the King's Road is mostly rained out
and a non-event.

V
An Alternate Take

Because of the rain
I was the entire pedestrian event
on King Street.

Gibbes Museum

I
Addie wants to go into the
comfortable pillow exhibit first.

II
The bicycling boys, 1838-42
William H. Johnson

One of them is a girl.
Also a cat or rabbit drawn cart.

III
Harriet Tubman, 1945
William H. Johnson

Harriet Tubman
is the real America.

IV
July Morning, 1940
Emil Armin

The kid looks happy but
this was long before July
had color.

V
Composition, 1940
Cleo Van Buskirk

A glimpse of color
in a black and white
room.

VI
Down to the Sea Again, 1935-39
Isabelle Greenberger

Everything in the sand
A sandwich
Ukulele
Smoking woman
Child with ice cream
A thin, thin man
Ample cleavage

VII
Two on a Bench, 1939
Eli Jacobi

They don't leave room
for a third.

VIII
Addie sees a bird and
flaps her way on in
to the next gallery.

IX
Sanctuary, 2020
Donté K. Hayes

Addie refers to this one as
The twenty boob-ed lady.
Upon further inspection
she thinks it's more like eighteen.

X
If you want pleasure
you must toil for it.

XI
Skillet Portrait Emma, 2002
Alison Saar

We do not have enough art
on the bottom of our
pots and pans.

XII
Lavender Notes, 2019
Stephanie J. Woods

The pillow head sisters.
Reunion tour.

XIII
Ms. Johnson, 1972
Barkley Hendricks

She's got a lot of extra room
on her green canvas
in case someone wants to
paint a man on.

XIV
Cobra Basket, 1983
Mary Jackson

Cobra not included.

XV
Self Portrait, 2001
Jill Hooper

That's why you only see one arm.
The other one is off canvas
doing the painting.

XVI
The Wreck of the Rose in Bloom, 1809
John Devaere

This will be us at the end of the trip –
Me carrying sleeping Addie
up the Blue Ridge Mountains.
Keep your shirt on, honey.

XVII
Accident, 1946
Jacob Lawrence

If everybody's leaning forward like that
an accident is bound to happen.

XVIII
April (The Green Gown), 1920
Childe Hassam

She looks bored with the painter.
I assure her it was worth the wait.

XIX
Maribou with Fish, 1934
Anna Hyatt Huntington

Three birds share a fish.
It looks like one is getting
a bigger piece.

XX
Three Green Fan Lady, 1912
Robert Henri

She looks serious.
And is my favorite.

XXI
Addie is tired but
when I tell her this
is the miniature gallery
I get an enthusiastic okay
and a walk on in.

XXII
Object Temporarily Removed, 2022

XXIII
Untitled (Hot Sauce, Louisiana), 1980
William Eggleston

Why not go ahead and call it
Hot Sauce, Louisiana?

XXIV
William Eggleston with gun, Memphis 1988
Maude Schuyler Clay

If I didn't know better
I'd say this was a youngish
Michael Constantine.

XXV
A candle in the gift shop
is scented *Damn Gina*
which smells nicer than you think.

Never Rain, Always Kittens

It is raining heavy in Charleston.
The kind of rain that could go on
for forty days. Addie's says

let's go to Basic Kitten, but means
Kitchen. There's nothing I'd like more
than to go to a basic kitten.

I want to keep it dry and let it know
I'm its friend. The water coming from
the sky, outside, will make everything difficult.

Thankfully the wine in this dry room
is making it easier for me to tolerate.
The rain has never been my friend.

Only kittens.

Bussing Basic Kitchen

The clinking of the glasses
on the bussing tray as he
carries it away to where they go
is unexpected music, ringing
through the lobby with rain drop
harmony.

Goodnight Charleston

Tonight, everyone in Charleston
at every restaurant talked with us
jumped in our pictures, and we in theirs.

We sat next to a couple in one place
where the husband was a music professor
like Addie, and the wife was a graphic designer

like Rick (that's me!) Our waitress became
another one of our best friends in her
three dollar thrift store customized shirt.

Another couple were repeat customers
and learned from us that you can go
to more than one city on your vacation.

(But I was very specific that it's okay
to spend more time in a city to really
get to know it.) Then we returned to

Magnolias for Pecan Pie and to try our luck
seeing Carrie who is a transplant,
who works the bar, and like most residents,

has yet to be a tourist in her own town.
Her person is a driver from over the sea.
Now we are all people who know each other

because when food and drink are involved
the camera shutters fly, social media
handles are easily exchanged.

It is good
to be a person
y'all.

Charleston
to Asheville

Good morning Charleston

It's going to be breakfast one more time in you.
You Boston of the south, or perhaps you like
to think of Boston as the you of *the north?*

There are things to buy and other things
to put in my suitcase after a last set of
footfalls occupies your heartbeat city market.

We weren't always on the same side but
if I forget thee, oh Charleston, may my
biscuit whither. May every time I encounter

moisture, it remind me of the water
in your air, and the body of it surrounding
your peninsula, pointing to the sea

where we all came from.

Observations

I
The Charleston Peninsula
looks a little bit like a
limp Florida.

II
Clouds over Charleston this morning
It knows we're leaving and it's
not happy about it.

III
The white noise machine in
our room has a *brook* setting
which, when turned up too loud
defeats the purpose.

Last Feet in Charleston

I
We see Hydie the cookie lady
one last time before our feet
leave Charleston's ground.
Every thing we see is one last
before a car takes us to another
car which takes us away.

II
We'll just have to
remember the bells and
the sound they make.

Car to Car

I
The driver tells us
he doesn't do this full time
which is what every Uber
or Lyft driver tells us.
No one will commit.

II
The Gullah ladies
at budget rental car
could care less that
we're in their lobby.

Drive to Asheville

I
Addie is delighted that you can
separately change the volume
of the navigation and of the music
on the car radio.

II
A sign tells us Cracker Barrel has
Cheesecake Pancakes which sounds like
death on a plate.

III
We drive by the Fruit of the Loom Factory.
Oh, underwear of my youth
I've brought you home.

IV
Jeff Cook
of Jeff Cook Real Estate
really wants me to know
how much my house is worth.

V
The roads out of Charleston are loud.
It may be a paving situation, though
later I realize our rental car is not that
premium and just may not have the
sound dampening technology
I am used to. My apologies, road,
for blaming you for the noise.

VI
The left lane has disappeared.
But it's okay, they told me it
was going to happen.

VII
The police cars
on Highway 26
are unmarked.
I think the trees
are in on it too.

VIII
We cross under 95 and could
easily turn right onto it and make our way
to Canada with a stop to visit Addie's family,
or left all the way to where Florida dangles out
into the ocean with a stop to visit mine.
We do neither and continue on to Asheville.

IX
I am reminded today is a work day
when I see a back hoe doing what
back hoes do.

X
Free tire pieces everywhere!

XI
A truck has the words
Building the Carolinas one load at a time
written on its back. Let's all assume
we know what this means.

XII
Addie is bored so I tell her to count the trees.
Every now and then she vocalizes a number,
but I'm not sure how accurate it is.

XIII
I got some color in the Charleston sun.
Unfortunately it's teal.

XIV
Months later I struggle with whether
haint wou;d have been funnier than *teal.*

XV
Our four hour drive takes us past
three *Historic Downtown* signs.
I'm sorry, historic downtowns of
South and North Carolina, the
Ethiopian food in Asheville
isn't going to eat itself.

XVI
The music shuffle brings on
Martin Luther King Jr.'s speech
at Temple Israel Of Hollywood.

It is longer than any song and
starts in the low country and
culminates with words about mountains

just as we start to ascend into the
Blue Ridge area. Martin reminds us
though the sites of slavery we toured

mere hours and days ago are
no longer active, our climb up
the mountain has not ended.

XVII
We're not in the low country anymore

Initial Ashevillisms

I
The Luperts have arrived in Asheville
is a message I've already sent to my
friends who seemed rather indifferent
about the whole affair.

II
We can tell, already,
Asheville has a type.

III
At the Kimpton Arrus Hotel
the elevators are in charge
and you just pray to God
they will take you to
your desired floor.

Billy's World

The Ethiopian food in Asheville
at the restaurant which almost

has Addie's name on it, is as good
as it should be, and made better

by the company – A *banger and sanger*
and his wife – the kind of people

the staff already know.
We retire to where a chicken coop

was built with bare hands and a local buddy.
The front gate will go up soon. You could

stand next to the coop at various
times of day and see badgers

coyote and bears. If you look up
a hawk. If you don't look up

you might just hear it.
The chickens are smarter

than one would assume.
They know where their home is.

They know where to lay their eggs.
They know to run under the porch

if hungry animals come by.
Nearby under the porch is the studio.

We get a treat in the form of a
one song concert just for us.

Every possible instrument is played.
Every possible instrument is played.

Billy's mind commits the spectacle
to muscle memory.

His new song will join a ritual
at a *Jubilee*. This is the kind of thing

that happens here. The kind of
genius thing. Though we think he

may be most proud of
the chicken coop.

Walking the Streets of Asheville Late at Night

Skeleton bench versus
naked meditator with two gnomes

The moon versus
chocolate fetish

Everything is closed and
the streets have a smell.

One man, part of the smell
is heard saying *we had a mandate.*

Permanent cats are
on a Cat Walk.

If there were donuts in site
this could easily be Portland.

The Portland of the south
though every place

deserves its own identity
so forget I said that.

Asheville
Day 1

From where I'm standing

it looks to Addie like I'm a lamp.
Have you met my husband the lobster
says Addie to Mr. Lamp.

Where The Streets Have Names

I
We walk by *The Lobster Trap*.
Addie's tells me *Don't get trapped
Mr. Lamp Lupert*.

II
We walk by a store called
Cute and Curious. Otherwise known
as the Addie wonderland of delights.

Two Graffitis in the Early Girl Cafe

I
*This toilet wishes
it was a bidet.*

II
*Kill all NAZIS.
Agreed.
Moo.*

The Biltmore Estate

I
Biltmore.
Built more.
They certainly did.

II
Because we like to know
what the *thing of things* is,
this is the Louvre of America.

III
A while down the driveway to the house
a sign tells you *two miles to the house.*
This is where we will driveway tonight!

IV
The fish in the Italian garden ponds
pop their whiskered heads up at us
as I wished the Dolphins did
at Tybee Island.

V
They have two billiard tables
in the billiard room. Man we
barely have space for one
in Newhall.

VI
In the banquet hall –
This is where we shall
Mother sleeping dine tonight

VII
Biltmore was thirty-five when
he moved in, and was single.
When I was thirty five
I was barely out of diapers
and hardly owned a shoe box.

VIII
The *more simple breakfast room*
could contain our entire house.

IX
We see a Monet in the salon
purchased by Biltmore
before Monet was famous.

X
Many of the National Gallery's
paintings were stored in the music room
during World War II.

Edith didn't charge anything for the storage
viewing it as a national service.

XI
I want to push
all the buttons
in the house.

XII
The tapestries took five years to plan
and another five to weave. If I took
that long to write a poem, you wouldn't
be reading this now.

XIII
The library contains a secret passageway
to the guest rooms which wasn't so secret
because they told everyone about it.

XIV
Atypically, paintings of the architect
and landscape architect hang
in the upstairs living space
showing respect for what they did.

XV
George's bedroom –
sorry Louis, is better than
yours in Versailles.

XVI
Addie wants to know why there's
so much seating in the bedroom.

XVII
George's treasured Rembrandt etchings
sit in the oak sitting room.

XVIII
Edith and George
we're married in Paris
at thirty-six
and twenty-five.

XIX
Forty
Three
Bathrooms

Only one bowling alley.

XX
It is doubtful, either in the old world or new, a
builder has ever erected a nobler residential edifice
than the southern home of Mr. George Vanderbilt.
~George Hill, Architectural record, 1885

XXI
The ladies dressing rooms didn't all have
full length mirrors, but more often than not
your ladies maid was dressing you and
she knew how you looked.

XXII
The indoor swimming pool has no windows
and looks like the kind of place where
slasher films might be set.

P.S. The pool leaks so it is not filled today.

XXIII
The showers in the fitness room
were needle showers which
doesn't sound like the kind
I want to use.

XXIV
The pantry cans are a sight
for the home edit crowd.

They're not in rainbow color order
Addie notices, and walks away

when I tell her rainbows
weren't invented until 1948

XXV
Addie tells me to get excited as we get to the bar room.
I tell her my readers are already very excited.
If you know Addie please contact her directly
to share your excitement about jars.

XXVI
No, Mr. Narrator –
My mouth is not watering
at the idea of meat rotating
in the rotisserie room.

XXVII
I think all dumb waiters need
is a little extra care.

XXVIII
I would a hundred percent
come down and dine with the servants
at least once a week.

Addie's not sure that would
have been allowed.

XXIX
Our visit continues in the smoking room.
Thankfully smoking is not allowed.

XXX
It's a surprise that there is also
a gun room.

XXXI
Remind me to plant cucumber leaf sunflowers.

XXXII
They have all the plants here.
All of them.

XXXIII
Touch
Look
Climb
Enjoy

Of these four words
we are only allowed to do two.

XXXIV
Addie tells a tree
I would like to touch you
but out of respect
doesn't.

XXXV
Addie's hot butt seat dance
off the uncomfortable sun heated
bench in the walled garden is
quite the performance and something
I'm wondering how to monetize.

XXXVI
As people approach the house
from the parking lotat which we are
arriving, I tell them *the butler did it* thus
saving them a lot of walking.

XXXVII
Addie sings along with the
seatbelt reminder sounds
which is something I may do
after the wine tasting.

XXXVIII
The site of ice cream has
given Addie new hope as we
navigate this hot day in
The Biltmore Estate.

XXXIX
We overhear people talking
about the wines they tried and liked.
But can we really trust those people?

XL
Our wine guy is *Adeeb* from Lebanon.

XLI
The gift shop has *traditional* cheese straws
which is nice but I'm looking for something more
out of the box when it comes to my
cheese straw intake.

XLII
Addie announces she would like
some cute forks and I don't think
it's just the wine talking until she
starts to pet me with the fluffy wallet.

XLIII
I slam a shatterproof wine glass
against my head and it does not shatter
thus proving the validity of that label.

XLIV
Wine tastings always make me happy.
I hope you've enjoyed the joy present
in the last few wine infused poems.

XLV
Napoleon's chess set –
One of the Vanderbilt's
prized possessions.

XLVI
At the last minute they decided
to sail on the Olympia
instead of the Titanic.

XLVII
I think Addie tells me they have grilled cheese
but she actually said malts and shakes so
I'm probably going to need to get everything
checked when I get home.

XLVIII
The direction we walk is
all depending on the
location of the chickens.

XLIX
A sign at the farm says
we should not chase animals
or other guests.

L
You guys are going to grow up
and be fine chickens I tell the little chicks.
Bock, adds Addie.

One Check

We drive to Nine Mile restaurant
outside of downtown which is not
nine miles away from here.

Later we'll draw a circle on a map
in a nine mile radius to determine
what the possibilities are.

One menu item says to *specify heat*
I'm planning on telling them *air conditioned*
and see how far that gets me.

I push my fork off the table.
Not intentionally. Later when she
takes the salad away, the fork falls off the plate.

This is the place of the jumping fork.
How far do they jump, Addie asks.
Nine miles she answers herself.

Someone at the next table mentions California.
I wonder if I, as a Californian, should offer to
weigh in on whatever they are talking about.

Addie would prefer I didn't.
Our server asks if we want one check?
We both slap our ring hands on the table

and say *yes please.*

Missing Context

I was going to say something
that began with *in a certain context*
but I don't remember what it was
and now the whole day is gone
and we'll never know what these
seventeen syllables were.

Asheville
Day 2

It May or May Not Rain

A lengthy conversation with the valet drivers
teaches us if it rains it may not last.
We'll learn long last if we can trust these people.
We're heading to donuts, one famous magazine
says is one of the best desserts in the country.
It helps that it's a food magazine whose name
in English means *good appetite*.
We have a good appetite and it has
been made clear to me, this morning
if we have donuts now, we're going to
need a *real lunch*. Everything is possible
this morning, except perhaps views
of the Blue Ridge Mountains, depending
on what the clouds and the rain decide to do.

In Hole

We're at a place called *Hole Donuts*
which is both delightful and alarming
depending on how you feel about holes.

Hole Tour

Addie peers through the window
to watch the process, a sign that says *Hole*
hanging over her shoulders.

They shape them, weigh them
fold them in the fryer.
I think a cookie cutter is involved

but I've lost track of the order.
The donut woman brings an order out
for Katherine who is not present.

I ask what's in the order as I
might be Katherine.
I've made everybody on west Asheville

laugh today. Oh, they flip the donuts
in the fryer. That's new information.
Addie says this place is *a hole in the wall.*

I'm not sure she understands
the gravity of what she's just said.
The glazing may be happening now.

The chocolate tour we were going to
go on later is sold out so Addie's self made
peer through the window tour

is not meant to be creepy. It's what
she's entitled to today. The donuts
are gathered using what Addie calls

a *donut stick.* The cinnamon sugar
takes longer and Addie's pantomime
of what the glazing machine does

is a once on a lifetime kind of performance.
The donuts are here. Excuse me,
I have to go.

doku

If these donuts were
the last thing I were to eat
It would be just fine.

Donut Lady

The donut lady knows Addie by name
and refers to her as their biggest fan.
They may be best friends now.

Is She Feeling Okay?

On the way to the Blue Ridge Parkway
we pass by *Discount Shoe Store*.
Addie doesn't say a thing.

Blue Ridge Parkway

I
We tried to *plan* a brief trip into the
Blue Ridge Parkway, but there was no need.
Every mile or so, there are overlooks

overlooking miles of mountains, and rivers.
You forget you are in America, especially if
like us, you live in Los Angeles or

a place like Los Angeles, where despite
the existence of mountains, and the ocean
there is so much infrastructure.

At Walnut Cove View Point, it`is so quiet.
Replace "Walnut Cove" with the names of
hundreds of other places to pull over

and these are the Blue Ridge Mountains.
So quiet - no infrastructure - except for the
road itself which makes it all so close.

We are not prepared for hiking as
attractive as the trailheads are, so we
are content with the distance.

II
Fork Mountain is not far from
Bad Fork Valley Overlook, so you
can imagine what happened here.

At Ultra Coffee

I
I ask him if there are any other choices
holding up the bag of Deep River Original
Sea Salt Chips, before I commit to these.
There are no other choices, he says so
this is, apparently, for life.

II
Addie needs another few spins
on the spinning stool before
she's ready to go.

River Arts District

I
One artist sells prints on the honor system.
The money-collecting box is empty
which could mean anything.

II
Sandi McAslan.
No relation.

III
Captain McWoof
is a painting of a dog
who is a captain
and dressed the part.

IV
It says *don't touch the artwork* everywhere
Is licking a form of touching?

V
Some paintings look like they're not finished
But that's more my problem than the artist's

VI
Rich Nelson's dog looks suspicious of us.

VI
We walk by *Integrative Family Medicine*
in the middle of the studios. D*o they
have a spleen on display,* I wonder.
Addie wants to know why
it's always about my spleen.
We'll have a whole session later
on the joy of the less popular
human organs.

VII
The font on the
Compact Car Parking Only sign
is quite compact.

VIII
Sandra says it took two hours
to do this painting –
Plus forty years.

IX
One artist says
*they didn't care much for you
on the French side of St. Martin,
if you didn't speak French.*
But she saw rainbows every day.
When you land, it is like
you are landing in the ocean.
When you leave, the planes
go straight up.

At Cultivated Cocktail

It's just the two of us
And little pours of different liquors
or spirits or tasty little beverages
in cute little glasses (ask me for photos)
we learn about *everything*.
Why rum?
Oh and then three half-cocktails
Cherry Garcia
I drunk.
Name of guy talking –
I don't know.
We're in a cage.
I would go with the 20% off
instead of the 10. In terms of
the coupons they gave us in our gift bag.

I don't finish the gin and tonic
But the Cherry Garcia cocktail –
This is a Solvang miniature horse situation.
I / we walk through the town,
with gift glasses, to dinner.
I drunk off my patootie.

Addie just told me to put my lip away.

Addie says the sink is too low
to the level of the sink.

What?

Ritual

Via Positiva

I am all kinds of cats
The hokey pokey.

One big circle —
Everybody's in it.

Via Negativa

The shadow comes to town.

All the instruments are
played again.

Via Creativa

Now pens and papers.
Our own shadows are
transcribed.

Via Transformativa

They made magic wands at
Camp Grandma and now we
wish for things we already have
so these wishes definitely come true.

Ritual

I am PayPal
I am give my cushion to the stranger
I am hokey pokey
I am in the one big circle
I am the shadow
I am still under the influence
I am need to leave
I am slow motion dead on the floor
I am grounded in the voices of
the young in the other room
I am ritual

New Character

A woman in Asheville emporium
tells us Addie looks like a character
out of a French film, not a pre-existing
character but a brand new one, Addie
in her cute, maybe French, dress.
Bien sur!

Late Night Delight

Later at night we stop for dessert
and french fries and it all comes with
cucumber slice in a glass of water.

At one point when I refill the water
the cucumber spins which, again,
delights Addie.

Our waitress is Petra who informs us
there are at least three other Petras
who live in town.

She is named after a branch higher up
on her tree, and not directly from the place
on the other side of the Jordan River.

I make jokes like her father. For example,
I ask if, knowing there are others,
is she *competrative*.

I finish the water, eat the cucumber.
Addie likes my cucumber water breath.
All of this is just to delight Addie.

Asheville to Charlotte

Waning Asheville

I don't know how you measure
the thickness of fog, but whatever
device is used, whatever scale it is
presented on, this would be impressive.

Asheville doesn't want us to leave.
Where is Highway 26, Highway 40?
It is impossible to know where
the roads are in this.

Okay Asheville, you win a couple
more hours from us. What breakfast
will you put inside is to entice us to stay?
Will your *Moogseum* seal the deal?

Will all the stops be tossed when you
present your chocolate store to us
named after the river we gazed upon
yesterday? Those sweet valet boys

who keep bringing us the car. I hate to
break it to them but this is going to be it.
You did your best, Asheville. I'm not saying
this is forever...Just for now.

Nothing But Clouds

The weather app says
partly cloudy but I don't think
it's looked outside where it
seems to be nothing but
cloudy.

I wore

very few of the fourteen t-shirts
I brought on this trip. Addie asks
if she can have a couple of them
so she can wrap up our souvenir
pint glasses. I tell her I was going
to wear all of them today which is
not the answer she was looking for.

Laila

Laila climbs on the tables
At the restaurant. Laila climbs
on her father at the restaurant.
She makes us rings in our preferred colors.
I'm happy to share my root hash
with Laila. Her smile could power
all of Asheville.

These Days

Every store on Lexington
sells incense and hemp products.
One used to sell watches.
But that was ten years ago.

Rock Spoons

The rock spoons at the *Center for Craft* gallery
each shaped like the rocks they hold
seem awfully specific in purpose.

Moogseum

I
When Bernie speaks
You got to eat
~Bootsy Collins

II
The moog
And the theremin
A *mootch* made in

...Moogven.

III
The theremin was one of the first
mass produced instruments.

IV
I didn't learn *how* to play the theremin
but I did learn how to have it make noise.

V
We turn electricity into sound
by turning knobs.

VI
Drone in D / E minor is technically
not a drone as it shifts back and forth
between Dm and Em.

VII
They offer complimentary tubes
if we want to take a poster home.
(We'd have to pay for the poster first.)

This song's for the fucking government

says the metal guitar player with voice to match
playing at the intersection on Central Square.
He's wearing headphones so we can only
hear his voice and not the guitar he is
singing along to. It'd be interesting to know
if he was any good.

We take Highway 40 to Charlotte.

If we took it the other way we could
go all the way to where it ends at
the 15 in California. (They call them
freeways there, and I believe *highways*
here, but perhaps the most inclusive
term is *interstate*.) At the 15 we could
turn left and go home, or right and
head to Las Vegas (though there's
a shortcut in Arizona.) The last time
I was on the 40 it was when I drove
Addie from Kansas City to Los Angeles.
The last time I thought about the word
interstate was in Hawaii where they,
have an interstate but it doesn't really
work as it is completely contained
within a single state. Perhaps that one
should be re-labeled intrastate. Anyway,
it is good to be back on the 40, or perhaps
they don't say *the* here? I am not an expert
in the language of the road, though I hear
in Los Angeles, they have forty words
for *asphalt*.

Bigger Loads

A sign on interstate 40, or perhaps
on a different road that we took once
we left interstate 40, said *Bigger loads
faster pay.* It sounds intriguing but
I'm not sure that's the business I
want to be in.

Slow Down, Please

It took us thirty eight minutes to fly from
Charlotte to Savannah. It took almost two
weeks to arrive back in Charlotte, from
Savannah. Both trips had their moments
but I prefer the latter.

There is a revolution of Singers at Oh My Soul in NoDa, Charlotte, North Carolina.

Dylan and Ella, the youngest of the bunch
perform on stage, twirling, dancing, and
occasionally throwing rocks. The number
of shoes they are wearing changes frequently.

This is not the first child we've seen today
wearing a suspect number of shoes.
Ella says *Mommy I love you*. She may
want something but she's too cute not
to have whatever it is.

Kim and Zach are the oldest of the Singers.
They eat meat and we're okay with that,
especially since they sent us a list of
vegetarian restaurants for us to choose from.
A lot of their focus is on wrangling the
younger Singers' dance performance.
That is simply to say they are parents
and this is how it is done.

They have two flavors of wings. One is
unreasonably spicy and not everyone realizes
that only one of them has these. All is revealed
after a wing exchange.

I start to answer different questions three times.
One about the Asheville ritual, one about
The Simpsons, and another, the topic of which
I forget. My answers trail off into the
younger Singers' dance performance.

They show must go on, for at least 18 years.
Probably more, if that's how you
parentally roll.

Toe Eyes

We dine at *Toe Eyes* restaurant
at the Singer compound.

Everything is pre-planned.
The salad, the single mushrooms.

The fact that we can pay using our phones
even though we were handed the

local currency prior to stopping in.
We don't have avocados says Ella.

She is the proprietor and has been
planning this for weeks.

The specialty is Cotton Candy Pizza
alarmingly, served with mushrooms.

We are offered veggie bacon and then
the restaurant is abandoned for

the drawing station. She draws a butterfly
and then everyone agrees next should be

a baby butterfly. Addie gets to sign her
name and Ella asks *what about the 'aunt' part.*

I'm not sure who has adopted who here
but both of them are on board.

No one knows what happened to the ears on
Ella's doll. No one really needs to know.

Two Final Cocktails

Who am I to sound so down?
We've still got biscuits
on the docket for tomorrow.

All You Need is Knowledge of
All You Need is Love

The man behind the Charlotte hotel desk
has never heard of the song *All You Need is Love.*
I want to say I'm feeling old but he's about my age.
I thought The Beatles was one of those groups
where everyone on Earth knew every one
of their songs. I'm glad to have put this one
on his radar, but it is me who has
learned something today.

Four Three Two Line Stanzas

The bartender smokes the cocktail
after it's been put in the glass which
our cocktail tour guide last night
would not have approved of.

It's okay, his double fisted shaking
mambo, plus the smoke drifting to
our table before the drinks arrive

let us know it will be an experience
no matter when the smoke was applied.

Charlotte to
Los Angeles

Good Morning Charlotte

Addie is packing. I am still in bed.
This is the normal order of things.

Soon I will not be in bed and
I will discover things that have been

placed in my suitcase. I will understand
the expectations of this and

no words will be spoken. Shortly
after this, we will have one more biscuit.

(each). This is the way of the south.
The blackout curtains have been opened.

This is a message to me.
It is time to move on.

Customize Your Clean

At the *Canopy by Hilton* in Charlotte
they say they will only clean your room
if you ask.

At the *Kimpton Brice Hotel* in Savannah
they say they will clean your room every day
but never do.

It's a different system.

The Multi-Book Pineapple Situation

I notice pineapple wallpaper at the coffee area
of our room. Pineapples are a sign of welcome
as I've mentioned earlier in this book, and, I think,
in another (Could have been *Donut Famine*
the book of poems I wrote in New Orleans.)
Is it strange to notice this on our last day?
Is there a symbol for goodbye? Is it an
upside down pineapple? Look for more
references to this in future books.

Still In the Room

By far the best blow dryer on the trip was at the *Hilton Canopy* hotel in Charlotte, North Carolina.

We Still Still Haven't Left the Room

I just noticed a pineapple painting in
another part of our hotel room.
Looks like you didn't have to wait for
the next book to hear about
pineapples again.

Ella Loves Addie

Ella begs to skip camp
so she can see us again.
Well, mostly Aunt Addie.

More On This Now

OMG there's a pineapple pillow too.
We're never leaving!

Mint Museum Uptown

I

I pretend to not be able to get back in
from the top floor terrace and tell Addie
one of us is going to have to eat the other.

II

Paintings from the 1700s next to
ones from the 2000s –
Art knows no era.

III

St Cecilia, a portrait
John Singleton Copley, 1748-1815

Her eyes pop out of the painting
and remind me of Dylan's.

IV

The people who painted their dogs
in the 1700s must really miss them.

V

Portrait of Isaac Gouverneur
Gilbert Stuart, 1793-1795

The service in this restaurant
is terrible.

VI

The Garden at Giverny
Mariquita Gill, circa 1895

Somehow Addie pronounced Giverny
in the original Yiddish.

VII
Moonlight
Elliot Dangerfield, 1915-1925

These are all the colors I need on a painting.

VIII
Adagio
Edward Middleton Manigault, 1912

Addie spots her people
in a painting. Sadly she can't
get in it with them, and they are
not available to come with us.

IX
Trumpet Flowers
Stanton Macdonald-Wright, 1919

Now Addie sees all the colors
she needs in a painting.

X
Joyous Life
Louis Loeb, 1902

Topless forest frolic.
Turns out Siri has a hard time
with the word topless.

XI
My Friend Brien
Robert Henri, 1913

Brien spells his name weird.

XII
Camouflage Man in a Landscape
James Guy, 1938

I'm distracted by
megaphone boob lady until
Addie shows me she's good at
camouflage and positions herself
to blend right in.

XIII
New Barn
Molly Luce, 1938

The horses are waiting
for the new barn to be finished
so they can go inside.

XIV
It's Never Too Late to Mend
Norman Rockwell, circa 1938

I make sure Addie sees the cat in this painting.
I look at her long and hard until she acknowledges.

XV
Shofar in the Stone
Theodoros Stamos, 1946

This was the alternative version of
the King Arthur tale.

Plus, I want to know if the artist
is related to John Stamos.

XVI
One room has art from the 1500s
in the same room as the 1970s.
Soon we'll see a painting from tomorrow
next to one made before creation.

XVII
Theories of Wisdom
Linda Foard Roberts, 2018

It's a foggy landscape. It's a butt.
It's a foggy landscape. It's a butt.
Hold on you two, it's both!

XVIII
Scotland
Grace Hartigan, 1960

This painting is at an angle and
I refuse to look at it until they fix it.

XIX
Addie pantomimes getting sucked into
one of the paintings and I tell her
that's how I lost my last wife.

XX
They stick some of the famous artists in the corners.
Warhol, Rockwell – Everyone has their place.

XXI
Sometimes I have the camera turned
the wrong way when I go to photograph
a piece of art and think *oh my god
that painting looks like me!*

XXII
The Mourners. My Last Family Photo, 1996

Single woman in polar bear suit sitting
in front of six conservatively dressed people.
Either one person or six people did not get
the dress code memo.

XXIII
Without Exception Everything is Reflected in This Mirror
Iruka Maria Toro, 2015-2016

This is a crazy game of *where's Suki.*

XXIV
Addie perks up a little bit when
she sees the sign that says
look for the touchable material tiles
in the galleries. Up until this point
she thought the vacation was over.

XXV
Metamorphosis VI
Stanislav Libensky, 1984-1987

Addie wants to put her head on this one
but there is no *please put your head on this one* tile.

XXVI
Bubble Wrap
Courtney Starret, 2008

I can't tell if it's bubble wrap
or *booble* wrap.

XXVII
White Ripple
Hoss Haley, 2013

It's a shame this one broke
before they installed it.

XXVIII
A man starts singing the scatting part of
Good Morning Starshine from *Hair* in the
middle of the staff art wing where, normally,
one would be quiet and just look at the art.
He approaches a sign which says please
do not go further and adds *or you will die.*
Addie wonders what I have to say about
any of this.

XXIX
I see a book called *How to Dress an Egg*
in the museum gift shop and I feel this is
gonna cost me a fortune in egg panties.

XXX
I see another book called *Why is Your Face.*
On page one it says *because it's preferable
to your butt.*

XXXI
A one-armed man holds the elevator for us.

Definitely Boundaries

A store in the airport is called *No Boundaries*.
It takes less than thirty seconds of my presence
in the store to learn that this is not true.

I Don't Remember This At All

Concourse C is where the cattle come
to be with each other. I am one of them today,
herded down the walkway waiting for my iced tea,
wondering why they're cheering at gate C5.
Moo. So much moo.

More Vacation Minutes

The plane as coming
The plane is delayed ten minutes
The plane is delayed an hour
The plane has landed
The plane is coming to the gate
The flight is delayed
The flight is delayed a week
The flight is delayed until
climate change changes
The plane and the flight
have not spoken for years
It's time to get off the plane
Not me, them.
The plane has lasagna on it
The lasagna is delayed
Here is the plane with the lasagna
Here is the plane
Who will operate the jetway
Who will open the door
Who will walk the walk
Where will they go
Who will greet them
Will they be okay
The plane is here
The plane

Notku

All the announcements
in terminal C are
passive aggressive.

Sayonara

Our flight crew may be Japanese
And they order the words they speak
in English as they might if it were
a different language. We are headed
to California, Los Angeles.
The doors are closed now.
Sayonara, Low Country.
Land of sweet tea and NASCAR
Of Billy Graham and biscuits.
Sayonara weird Asheville.
That's your term, not an insult.
Sayonara, y'all.
Until we meet again.

Nearby Lasagna

Charlotte is an *American* hub.
American is a Charlotte hub.
I'm a hubber not a flighter.
There is a plane pointing at me.
Now two. Now taxi. I taxi with
nearby lasagna.

Memory

Once I got in trouble for
bungee jumping on live radio.
The program director scolded me
about liability, but then asked if
it was fun. There was a video tape
of it that I never got to see.
I remember feeling weightless
for a moment after the first bounce.
I'm not sure why I'm thinking of this now
as the wheels of this plane
leave the Charlotte ground.

I Have My Limits

The tallest building in Uptown Charlotte
has lots of spiky sharp points.
I like to look at it but I'd hate to fall
on it from the sky above.

Flying Home

I
It will be a while
before I'll feel like eating
a biscuit again.

II
These clouds look like
snow biscuits.

III
They give us hot nuts in the plane.
Addie remembers they had hot towels
on the previous flight and I tell her
they're only allowed one hot thing
on the flight, towels or nuts.
She says she would have liked to
wash her hands before eating hot nuts
and then pauses and says or *anything*...

Rick Lupert will return
unless Mt. Vesuvius isn't quite
as dormant as everybody thinks.

About The Author

The author with his people in Savannah

Three-time Pushcart Prize, and Best of the Net nominee Rick Lupert has been involved with poetry in Los Angeles since 1990. He was awarded the Beyond Baroque Distinguished Service Award in 2014 for service to the Los Angeles poetry community. He served for two years as a co-director of the non-profit literary organization Valley Contemporary Poets. His poetry has appeared in numerous magazines and literary journals, including *The Los Angeles Times, Rattle, Chiron Review, Red Fez, Zuzu's Petals, Stirring, The Bicycle Review, Caffeine Magazine, Blue Satellite* and others. He edited the anthologies *A Poet's Siddur: Shabbat Evening - Liturgy Through the Eyes of Poets, Ekphrastia Gone Wild - Poems Inspired by Art, A Poet's Haggadah: Passover through the Eyes of Poets*, and *The Night Goes on All Night - Noir Inspired Poetry*, and is the author of twenty-six other books: *I Am Not Writing a Book of Poems in HAwaii, The Tokyo-Van Nuys Express, Hunka Hunka Howdee!, 17 Holy Syllables, God Wrestler: A Poem for Every Torah Portion*, (Ain't Got No Press) *Beautiful Mistakes, Donut Famine, Romancing the Blarney Stone, Professor Clown on Parade, Making Love to the 50 Ft. Woman, The Gettysburg Undress (Rothco Press), Nothing in New England is New, Death of a Mauve Bat, Sinzibuckwud!, We Put Things In Our Mouths, Paris: It's The Cheese, I Am My Own Orange County, Mowing Fargo, I'm a Jew. Are You?, Feeding Holy Cats, Stolen Mummies, I'd Like to Bake Your Goods, A Man With No Teeth Serves Us Breakfast* (Ain't Got No Press), *Lizard King of the Laundromat, Brendan Constantine is My Kind of Town* (Inevitable Press) and *Up Liberty's Skirt* (Cassowary Press), and the spoken word album *Rick Lupert Live and Dead* (Ain't Got No Press). He hosted the long running Cobalt Café reading series in Canoga Park for almost twenty-one years, relaunched in 2020 as a virtual series, and has read his poetry all over the world.

Rick created *Poetry Super Highway*, an online resource and publication for poets (PoetrySuperHighway.com), *Haikuniverse*, a daily online small poem publication (Haikuniverse.com), and writes and occasionally draws the daily web comic *Cat and Banana* with Brendan Constantine. (facebook.com/catandbanana) He also writes a weekly Jewish poetry column for the Los Angeles Jewish Journal.

Rick works as a music teacher at synagogues in Southern California and as a graphic and web designer for anyone who would like to help pay his mortgage.

Rick's Other Books and Recordings

I Am Not Writing a Book of Poems in Hawaii
Ain't Got No Press ~ August, 2022
The Tokyo-Van Nuys Express
Ain't Got No Press ~ August, 2020
Hunka Hunka Howdee!
Ain't Got No Press ~ May, 2019
Beautiful Mistakes
Rothco Press ~ May, 2018
17 Holy Syllables
Ain't Got No Press ~ January, 2018

A Poet's Siddur: Friday Evening (edited by)
Ain't Got No Press ~ November, 2017
God Wrestler: A Poem for Every Torah Portion
Ain't Got No Press ~ August, 2017
Donut Famine
Rothco Press ~ December, 2016
Romancing the Blarney Stone
Rothco Press ~ December, 2016
Professor Clown on Parade
Rothco Press ~ December, 2016

Rick Lupert Live and Dead (Album)
Ain't Got No Press ~ March, 2016
Making Love to the 50 Ft. Woman
Rothco Press ~ May, 2015
The Gettysburg Undress
Rothco Press ~ May, 2014
Ekphrastia Gone Wild (edited by)
Ain't Got No Press ~ July, 2013
Nothing in New England is New
Ain't Got No Press ~ March, 2013
Death of a Mauve Bat
Ain't Got No Press ~ January, 2012

The Night Goes On All Night Noir Inspired Poetry
(edited by)
Ain't Got No Press ~ November, 2011
Sinzibuckwud!
Ain't Got No Press ~ January, 2011
We Put Things In Our Mouths
Ain't Got No Press ~ January, 2010
A Poet's Haggadah (edited by)
Ain't Got No Press ~ April, 2008

A Man With No Teeth Serves Us Breakfast
Ain't Got No Press ~ May, 2007
I'd Like to Bake Your Goods
Ain't Got No Press ~ January, 2006
Stolen Mummies
Ain't Got No Press ~ February, 2003
Brendan Constantine is My Kind of Town
Inevitable Press ~ September, 2001
Up Liberty's Skirt
Cassowary Press ~ March, 2001

Feeding Holy Cats
Cassowary Press ~ May, 2000
I'm a Jew, Are You?
Cassowary Press ~ May, 2000
Mowing Fargo
Sacred Beverage Press ~ December, 1998
Lizard King of the Laundromat
The Inevitable Press ~ February, 1998
I Am My Own Orange County
Ain't Got No Press ~ May, 1997
Paris: It's The Cheese
Ain't Got No Press ~ May, 1996

For more information:
www.PoetrySuperHighway.com

CPSIA information can be obtained
at www.ICGtesting.com
Printed in the USA
JSHW012042100523
41553JS00005B/253

9 781733 027830